Bond

Fifth papers

11+–12+ years

Michellejoy Hughes

Comprehension

OXFORD
UNIVERSITY PRESS

Great Clarendon Street, Oxford, OX2 6DP, United Kingdom

Oxford University Press is a department of the University of Oxford.
It furthers the University's objective of excellence in research, scholarship,
and education by publishing worldwide. Oxford is a registered trade mark of
Oxford University Press in the UK and in certain other countries

First published by Nelson Thornes Ltd in 2009
This edition published by Oxford University Press in 2014

British Library Cataloguing in Publication Data
Data available

978-1-4085-0402-4

6

Printed in China

Acknowledgements

Illustrations: Angela Knowles
Page make-up: Pantek Arts Ltd, Maidstone, Kent

Extract from *The Talisman* by Sir Walter Scott, sourced from www.gutenberg.org;
Extract from *Hard Times* by Charles Dickens, sourced from www.gutenberg.org;
Extract from *Pilgrim's Progress* by John Bunyan, sourced from www.ccel.org; Extract
from *Frankenstein* by Mary Shelley, sourced from www.gutenberg.org;
Extract from *Richard III* by William Shakespeare, sourced from www.gutenberg.org;
Extract from *The Lady of Shalott* by Alfred Lord Tennyson, sourced from
www.poetry-online.org; Extract from *The Moonstone* by Wilkie Collins, sourced
from www.gutenberg.org; Extract from *The Awakening of Europe* by M. B. Synge,
sourced from www.mainlesson.com.

Although we have made every effort to trace and contact all
copyright holders before publication this has not been possible in all
cases. If notified, the publisher will rectify any errors or omissions at
the earliest opportunity.

Before you get started

About Bond

Bond is the leading name in practice for 11+ and other selective school exams (e.g. 7+, 12+, 13+, CEE), as well as for general practice in key learning skills. The series provides resources across the 5–13 years age range for English and maths and 6–12 years for verbal reasoning and non-verbal reasoning. Bond's English resources are also ideal preparation for teacher assessments at Key Stages 1 and 3, as well as for Key Stage 2 SATs.

About comprehension

Comprehension is a vital life skill. It involves the ability to critically read and understand written material and then to take or use relevant information from it. This skill is developed in children from an early age; consequently comprehension exercises form a core component of most English exams and assessments in school.

To test the breadth of a child's comprehension ability, exams may present one or more extracts taken from works of fiction (i.e. novels), poetry, playscripts or non-fiction (i.e. biographies, leaflets, advertisements, newspaper and magazine articles). Questions are likely to range from those that require direct, literal answers (e.g. 'What colour was the girl's coat?') to those that, with increasing levels of complexity, involve inferring information and offering a personal opinion (e.g. 'Why did Tom decide to put the money back?'; 'How do you think he felt when he realised that the money had gone?').

Children are likely to face a range of different comprehension tasks throughout Key Stages 1–3, particularly in English end-of-year assessments, Key Stage 2 SATs and 11+ (as well as other selective) English exams. Both wide reading and regular, focused comprehension practice are therefore essential for success.

What does the book contain?

- **10 papers** – providing comprehension practice in fiction, non-fiction and poetry. Each test includes one or more passages to read, followed by questions. The number of questions in a paper may vary but each test is worth a total of 35 marks. The comprehension texts and questions have been pitched at the level of a typical 11+ exam.

- **Tutorial links** throughout – 📖 – this icon appears in the margin next to the questions. It indicates links to the relevant sections in *The secrets of Comprehension*, our invaluable guide that explains all key aspects of comprehension.

- **Scoring devices** – there are score boxes in the margins and a Progress Chart on page 52.

- **Answers** – located in an easily-removed central pull-out section.

How can you use this book?

Flexibility is one of the great strengths of the Bond series. These comprehension books can therefore be used at home, in school and by tutors to:

- set timed exercises – for each paper allow around 10 minutes to read the extract(s), followed by 30 minutes to answer the questions; this will provide good practice for 11+ (and other exam) time frames
- provide regular, bite-sized practice
- highlight strengths and weaknesses
- identify individual needs
- set homework
- help build a complete 11+ English preparation strategy alongside other Bond resources (see below).

It is best to start at the beginning and work through the papers in order. If you are using the book as part of a careful 11+ preparation plan, we suggest that you also have these other Bond resources close at hand:

The secrets of Comprehension: this practical handbook is an essential support for *Bond Comprehension 11+–12+ years*. *The secrets of Comprehension* clearly explains to children how to read and understand a text, how to approach the core question types and how to assess their own answers. The margin icons in *Bond Comprehension 11+–12+ years* indicate which questions are cross-referenced to the relevant sections of this handbook.

Bond Assessment Papers in English: these graded books provide lots of timed practice at comprehension, spelling, grammar and vocabulary work, in line with the scope of 11+ (and other) English exams.

How to do … 11+ English: the subject guide that explains all aspects of 11+ English.

The Parents' Guide to the 11+: the step-by-step guide to the whole 11+ experience. It clearly explains the 11+ process, provides guidance on how to assess a child and helps you to set a complete action plan for a strategic run-in to the exam.

See the inside front cover for more details of these books.

What does a child's score mean and how can it be improved?

It is unfortunately impossible to guarantee that a child will pass the 11+ English exam (or any comprehension test) if they achieve a certain score on a practice paper. Success on the day will depend on a host of factors, including the performance of the other children. However, we can give some guidance on what a score indicates and how to improve it.

If children colour in the Progress Chart (page 52), this will give an indication of performance in percentage terms. The Next Steps Planner inside the back cover will then help you to decide what to do next. It is always valuable to go over incorrect answers with children. If they are having trouble with any particular question type, follow the tutorial links to *The secrets of Comprehension* for step-by-step explanations and further practice.

Don't forget the website…!

Visit www.bond11plus.co.uk for lots of free resources, advice and information about Bond, the 11+ and helping children to do their best.

Key words

adjective	a word that describes somebody or something
alliteration	a repetition of the same sound *five funny frogs*
metaphor	an expression in which something is described in terms usually associated with another *the sky is a <u>sapphire sea</u>*
monologue	a long speech given by one person
narrator	a person who is telling a story
personification	a way of describing something that is not human by giving it human characteristics *the flowers <u>smiled</u> as they <u>nodded</u> in the breeze*
simile	an expression to describe what something is like *as cold as ice*
synonym	a word with the same or very similar meaning to another word *quick – fast*
verb	a 'doing' or 'being' word

The burning sun of Syria had not yet attained its highest point in the horizon, when a knight of the Red Cross, who had left his distant northern home and joined the host of the Crusaders in Palestine, was pacing slowly along the sandy deserts which lie in the vicinity of the Dead Sea, or, as it is called, the Lake Asphaltites, where the waves of the Jordan pour themselves into an inland sea, from which there is no discharge of waters.

The warlike pilgrim had toiled among cliffs and precipices during the earlier part of the morning. More lately, issuing from those rocky and dangerous defiles, he had entered upon that great plain, where the accursed cities provoked, in ancient days, the direct and dreadful vengeance of the Omnipotent.

The toil, the thirst, the dangers of the way, were forgotten, as the traveller recalled the fearful catastrophe which had converted into an arid and dismal wilderness the fair and fertile valley of Siddim, once well watered, even as the Garden of the Lord, now a parched and blighted waste, condemned to eternal sterility.

Crossing himself, as he viewed the dark mass of rolling waters, in colour as in duality unlike those of any other lake, the traveller shuddered as he remembered that beneath these sluggish waves lay the once proud cities of the plain, whose grave was dug by the thunder of the heavens, or the eruption of subterraneous fire, and whose remains were hid, even by that sea which holds no living fish in its bosom, bears no skiff on its surface, and, as if its own dreadful bed were the only fit receptacle for its sullen waters, sends not, like other lakes, a tribute to the ocean. The whole land around, as in the days of Moses, was 'brimstone and salt; it is not sown, nor beareth, nor any grass groweth thereon.' The land as well as the lake might be termed dead, as producing nothing having resemblance to vegetation, and even the very air was entirely devoid of its ordinary winged inhabitants, deterred probably by the odour of bitumen and sulphur which the burning sun exhaled from the waters of the lake in steaming clouds, frequently assuming the appearance of waterspouts. Masses of the slimy and sulphureous substance called naphtha, which floated idly on the sluggish and sullen waves, supplied those rolling clouds with new vapours, and afforded awful testimony to the truth of the Mosaic history.

Upon this scene of desolation the sun shone with almost intolerable splendour, and all living nature seemed to have hidden itself from the rays, excepting the solitary figure which moved through the flitting sand at a foot's pace, and appeared the sole breathing thing on the wide surface of the plain. The dress of the rider and the accoutrements of his horse were peculiarly unfit for the traveller in such a country. A coat of linked mail, with long sleeves, plated gauntlets, and a steel breastplate, had not been esteemed a sufficient weight of armour; there were also his triangular shield suspended round his neck, and his barred helmet of steel, over which he had a hood and collar of mail, which was drawn around the warrior's shoulders and throat, and filled up the vacancy between the hauberk and the headpiece. His lower limbs were sheathed, like his body, in flexible mail, securing the legs and thighs, while the feet rested in plated shoes, which corresponded with the gauntlets. A long, broad, straight-shaped, double-edged falchion, with a handle formed like a cross, corresponded with a stout poniard on the other side. The knight also bore, secured to his saddle, with one end resting on his stirrup, the long steel-headed lance, his own proper weapon, which, as he rode, projected backwards, and displayed its little pennoncelle, to dally with the faint breeze, or drop in the dead calm.

From *The Talisman* by Sir Walter Scott

Answer these questions.

1 Tick the TWO statements that are true.

A The knight was completing his journey on foot. ☐

B Thriving cities could be found beneath Lake Asphaltites. ☐

C It was midday when the knight was pacing slowly across the desert. ☐

D The knight's journey to reach the lake had not been easy. ☐

E The knight saw no birds in the sky. ☐

2 Give THREE possible reasons for why the traveller was 'pacing slowly' (line 3).

_____

_____

_____

_____

3 From the information given in the text, who, or what, do you think the word 'Omnipotent' is referring to (line 10)?

_____

4 Why do you think that the traveller 'crossed himself' as he reached the waters (line 15)?

_____

_____

5 Has the landscape always looked as it does now? Support your answer with evidence from the text.

_____

_____

_____

_____

6 How does the author create such a vivid picture of the landscape? Refer to the text in your answer.

B 2

_____

_____

_____

_____

_____

4

7 Explain in your own words, TWO possible causes of the 'fearful catastrophe' (line 12).

B 2

_____

_____

2

8 Describe, in your own words, why the knight and his companion seemed 'peculiarly unfit for the traveller in such a country' (lines 35–36).

B 2

_____

_____

_____

_____

3

9 What do you think is meant by each of these words as they are used in the text?

B 2

a subterraneous (line 18) _____   **b** accursed (line 9) _____

c stout (line 44) _____   **d** sheathed (line 41) _____

4

10 What do you think a 'falchion' is (line 43)?

B 2

_____

1

11 Explain the following phrases, as they are used in the text.

B 2

a '...the sun shone with almost intolerable splendour...' (line 31)

_____

_____

b '...to dally with the faint breeze...' (line 47)

_____

_____

c '…floated idly on the sluggish and sullen waves…' (line 29)

_____

_____

⬤ 3

12 Why do you think that Lake Asphaltites is also referred to as the Dead Sea (line 4)? Support your answer with THREE pieces of evidence from the text.

B 2

_____

_____

_____

_____

⬤ 3

13 What type of source do you think this extract has been taken from? Explain your answer with reference to the text.

B 1

_____

_____

_____

_____

_____

_____

⬤ 4

14 A 'talisman' is a good luck charm. Explain why this might be an effective title for this text.

B 2

_____

_____

_____

_____

_____

_____

⬤ 2

Now go to the Progress Chart to record your score!   Total ⬤ 35

Paper 2

Extract from Chapter I

'NOW, what I want is, Facts. Teach these boys and girls nothing but Facts. Facts alone are wanted in life. Plant nothing else, and root out everything else. You can only form the minds of reasoning animals upon Facts: nothing else will ever be of any service to them. This is the principle on which I bring up my own children, and this is the principle on which I bring up these children. Stick to Facts, sir!'   5

The scene was a plain, bare, monotonous vault of a school-room, and the speaker's square forefinger emphasized his observations by underscoring every sentence with a line on the schoolmaster's sleeve. The emphasis was helped by the speaker's square wall of a forehead, which had his eyebrows for its base, while his eyes found commodious cellarage in two dark caves, overshadowed by the wall.   10
The emphasis was helped by the speaker's mouth, which was wide, thin, and hard set. The emphasis was helped by the speaker's voice, which was inflexible, dry, and dictatorial. The emphasis was helped by the speaker's hair, which bristled on the skirts of his bald head, a plantation of firs to keep the wind from its shining surface, all covered with knobs, like the crust of a plum pie, as if the head had scarcely   15
warehouse-room for the hard facts stored inside. The speaker's obstinate carriage, square coat, square legs, square shoulders, – nay, his very neckcloth, trained to take him by the throat with an unaccommodating grasp, like a stubborn fact, as it was, – all helped the emphasis.

'In this life, we want nothing but Facts, sir; nothing but Facts!'   20

The speaker, and the schoolmaster, and the third grown person present, all backed a little, and swept with their eyes the inclined plane of little vessels then and there arranged in order, ready to have imperial gallons of facts poured into them until they were full to the brim.

Extract from Chapter II

'Very well,' said this gentleman, briskly smiling, and folding his arms. 'That's   25
a horse. Now, let me ask you girls and boys, Would you paper a room with representations of horses?'

After a pause, one half of the children cried in chorus, 'Yes, sir!' Upon which the other half, seeing in the gentleman's face that Yes was wrong, cried out in chorus, 'No, sir!' – as the custom is, in these examinations.   30

'Of course, No. Why wouldn't you?'

A pause. One corpulent slow boy, with a wheezy manner of breathing, ventured the answer, Because he wouldn't paper a room at all, but would paint it.

'You must paper it,' said the gentleman, rather warmly.

'You must paper it,' said Thomas Gradgrind, 'whether you like it or not. Don't tell   35
us you wouldn't paper it. What do you mean, boy?'

'I'll explain to you, then,' said the gentleman, after another and a dismal pause, 'why you wouldn't paper a room with representations of horses. Do you ever see horses walking up and down the sides of rooms in reality – in fact? Do you?'

'Yes, sir!' from one half. 'No, sir!' from the other. 40

'Of course no,' said the gentleman, with an indignant look at the wrong half. 'Why, then, you are not to see anywhere, what you don't see in fact; you are not to have anywhere, what you don't have in fact. What is called Taste, is only another name for Fact.' Thomas Gradgrind nodded his approbation.

'This is a new principle, a discovery, a great discovery,' said the gentleman. 'Now, 45 I'll try you again. Suppose you were going to carpet a room. Would you use a carpet having a representation of flowers upon it?'

There being a general conviction by this time that 'No, sir!' was always the right answer to this gentleman, the chorus of NO was very strong. Only a few feeble stragglers said Yes: among them Sissy Jupe. 50

'Girl number twenty,' said the gentleman, smiling in the calm strength of knowledge.

Sissy blushed, and stood up.

'So you would carpet your room – or your husband's room, if you were a grown woman, and had a husband – with representations of flowers, would you?' said the 55 gentleman. 'Why would you?'

'If you please, sir, I am very fond of flowers,' returned the girl.

'And is that why you would put tables and chairs upon them, and have people walking over them with heavy boots?'

'It wouldn't hurt them, sir. They wouldn't crush and wither, if you please, sir. They 60 would be the pictures of what was very pretty and pleasant, and I would fancy –'

'Ay, ay, ay! But you mustn't fancy,' cried the gentleman, quite elated by coming so happily to his point. 'That's it! You are never to fancy.'

'You are not, Cecilia Jupe,' Thomas Gradgrind solemnly repeated, 'to do anything of that kind.' 65

'Fact, fact, fact!' said the gentleman. And 'Fact, fact, fact!' repeated Thomas Gradgrind.

'You are to be in all things regulated and governed,' said the gentleman, 'by fact. We hope to have, before long, a board of fact, composed of commissioners of fact, who will force the people to be a people of fact, and of nothing but fact. You must 70 discard the word Fancy altogether. You have nothing to do with it. You are not to have, in any object of use or ornament, what would be a contradiction in fact. You don't walk upon flowers in fact; you cannot be allowed to walk upon flowers in carpets. You don't find that foreign birds and butterflies come and perch upon your crockery; you cannot be permitted to paint foreign birds and butterflies upon your 75 crockery. You never meet with quadrupeds going up and down walls; you must not have quadrupeds represented upon walls. You must use,' said the gentleman, 'for all these purposes, combinations and modifications (in primary colours) of mathematical figures which are susceptible of proof and demonstration. This is the new discovery. This is fact. This is taste.' 80

From *Hard Times* by Charles Dickens

1 Why do you think that the author repeats the phrase, '...the emphasis was helped by...' several times in Chapter I?

B 2

_____

_____

2

2 Which literary technique is the following an example of?

B 2

'...overshadowed by the wall...' (line 10) _____

1

3 Imagine that you are one of the children in Chapter I. Describe, in your own words, the room you are sitting in and the person who is speaking.

B 2

_____

_____

_____

_____

_____

_____

_____

_____

8

4 Look again at lines 1–5. Give an example of where the author uses imagery of nature.

B 2

_____

_____

2

5 Explain what is meant by the following phrases.

B 2

a '...You can only form the minds of reasoning animals upon Facts...' (lines 2–3)

_____

_____

b '...smiling in the calm strength of knowledge...' (lines 51–52)

_____

_____

2

6 Which two-word phrase is used for the remaining pupils who have not learnt the correct response to 'the gentleman's' questions?

_____

7 Find TWO examples of where the author has used a **simile** in the text.

_____

_____

8 Give the roots of the following words.

    a modifications _____   **b** unaccommodating _____

9 What does the way in which 'the gentleman' refers to Cecilia Jupe, tell you about his relationship with the children? Refer to the text in your answer.

_____

_____

_____

10 Which one word or short phrase, as used in the text, means the same as:

    a posture _____   **b** droop _____

    c eliminate _____   **d** angry _____

11 Why do you think that 'the gentleman' was so pleased by Cecilia's response?

_____

_____

12 What does 'the gentleman' mean when he states, 'This is fact. This is taste'? (line 80)

_____

_____

13 'The gentleman' would find red and white vertically-striped wallpaper acceptable. Do you agree with this statement? Refer to the text in your answer.

_____

_____

_____

_____

B 2

1

B 2

2

B 2

2

B 2

2

B 2

4

B 2

2

B 2

1

B 2

3

14 This extract is not taken from a modern text. Find THREE examples of words or short phrases that support this statement.

_____

_____

3

_____

Now go to the Progress Chart to record your score!　　Total　　35

Extract A

The Caribbean

General background

The Caribbean Islands cover an area in excess of 2,500 miles in length by 160 miles
wide. They are an archipelago, or chain of islands, which contains thousands of
islands, reefs (layers of rock, sand or shingle lying just on or below the surface of the   5
sea) and cays (low lying islands made from sand and corals). Each habited island has
a language and culture of its own; from the Dutch-speaking **Aruba** and the French-
speaking **Haiti**, to the English-speaking **Barbados**. On several islands, such as
Jamaica, you will also find many locals conversing in their native **Creole**.

The traditional exports from the Caribbean have been aluminium, bananas, oil,   10
oxides, rum and sugar. The Caribbean area represents 10 per cent of the world's
population but, in terms of **gross domestic product**, the Caribbean only has 3 per cent
of the wealth with **Dominica** being listed as the third poorest place. (It was ranked 176th
out of 179 countries in terms of wealth by the International Monetary Fund.) The region
is placed in the line of many major shipping routes with the Panama Canal connecting   15
the Pacific Ocean with the Caribbean Sea. The fringe of the Atlantic Ocean is just north
of the island of **Puerto Rico** – the deepest point in the whole of the Atlantic.

Landscape and climate

Some of the islands have quite a flat terrain whereas other islands have soaring
mountain ranges. The islands have a mixture of volcanic and non-volcanic origins and,   20
although the climate for this region is tropical, it experiences a wide range of weather
conditions. The moist, warm trade winds from the east help to create a rainforest on the
more mountainous islands, whereas the islands in the far west are kept drier. It is true
that the Caribbean is susceptible to hurricanes but these are restricted to certain times
of the year – travel agencies or tourism web sites can keep the prospective visitor up to   25
date on the likelihood of hurricanes hitting particular islands.

Of course, the Caribbean is especially renowned for its glorious marine life, so divers
and snorkellers often find themselves in paradise. Migratory schools of fish, the coral
reef and inquisitive turtles are just some of the amazing highlights that can be seen.
It isn't just sea creatures that make the Caribbean a delightful place to visit though.   30
The area is also known throughout the world as a biodiversity hotspot. The diverse
ecosystems of cactus scrublands and forested areas are home to so many threatened
species; from the giant shrews to the Cuban crocodile. Numerous birds, mammals
and reptiles, some of them on the brink of extinction, can be found on many of the
Caribbean islands.   35

Holiday appeal

The Caribbean has been a popular holiday destination for many years and offers
something for everyone. Choosing a particular island as a holiday base may be the
visitor's only difficulty! Sporty, active types will love the huge range of water sports
available; from white-water rafting and some of the world's best diving spots that   40

Antigua can offer, to **Martinique**'s fabulous shipwreck adventures. Families will be attracted to the safe, shallow waters and quiet island life found on **Grenada** and by **Guadeloupe**'s rainforest adventures for young explorers. Culture vultures can explore the Spanish-speaking **Dominican Republic** (it was Spain's first city of the New World), or the carnivals and traditional music of **Trinidad**. Of course, if guests wish to enjoy the best of all of these Caribbean features, then they can't go far wrong by choosing **Barbados** or **Jamaica**. One thing is for sure; visitors rarely regret taking a Caribbean holiday, which is why so many people return to the islands year after year.

45

(For more information on the history of the Caribbean Islands, see pages 80–95.)

Extract B

Commissioner General: 11/03/2009
FAO: Circulate to all UK travel agents
Ref: Safety & Security

A Caribbean vacation, whilst an excellent choice for holidaymakers, does have a reputation regarding safety and security. It is of vital importance that a travel health professional is consulted a month or so before departure to ensure the correct immunization and malaria recommendations are received. Early immunization is necessary but other safety precautions should also be taken. For example, protective clothing and DEET insect repellent are vital, as are bed nets in all sleeping areas.

5

We also advise you to draw the following safety tips top ten to the attention of anyone wishing to visit the Caribbean:

10

1. Never travel after daylight hours.
2. Avoid using unregistered or unmarked taxis.
3. Never swim in water that is not salt water or has not been well chlorinated.
4. ALWAYS use purified water – even when cleaning teeth; ice cubes in drinks should be avoided.
5. Remember the consummation rule: Peel it, Boil it or Forget it!
6. Avoid riding motorcycles.
7. Refrain from walking barefoot – cuts can easily become infected in the tropics.
8. Ensure that any medications are easily accessible in hand luggage.
9. Pack a first aid kit.
10. Take out emergency medical insurance in addition to a standard travel insurance policy.

15

20

The total average murder rate in the Caribbean last year was 3 people in every 10,000; 4 times higher than in the USA and 34 times higher than in the UK. Islands such as Monserrat, the Cayman Islands, St Bart, Bonaire, Dominica and the British Virgin Islands record far less criminal activity; Jamaica, Barbados, the US Virgin Islands, The Dominican Republic and Puerto Rico have higher rates. In general, the most affluent islands, or those that have the least tourism, are the safest, while those islands with high rates of unemployment and limited economic development often fall prey to narcotic trafficking, violence, gang-related crimes and incidences of theft. Generally, tourists are more likely than the islanders to find themselves targets for theft.

25

30

These facts should not dissuade visitors from travelling to the Caribbean, but should encourage them to take standard security steps seriously.

Extract C

At-a-glance figures:

	Lowest average temp.	Highest average temp.	Rainy season												
Aruba	81°	85°	J	F	M	A	M	J	J	A	S	**O**	**N**	**D**
Barbados	79°	82°	J	F	M	A	M	**J**	**J**	**A**	**S**	**O**	**N**	D
Cuba	72°	81°	J	F	M	A	**M**	**J**	**J**	**A**	**S**	**O**	N	D
Dominica	82°	82°	J	F	M	A	M	**J**	**J**	**A**	**S**	**O**	**N**	D
Grenada	73°	81°	J	F	M	A	M	**J**	**J**	**A**	**S**	**O**	**N**	D
Haiti	77°	83°	J	F	M	A	M	**J**	**J**	**A**	**S**	**O**	**N**	**D**
Jamaica	80°	85°	J	F	M	**A**	**M**	J	J	**A**	**S**	**O**	N	D
St Vincent	75°	87°	J	F	M	A	M	J	**J**	**A**	**S**	**O**	N	D
Trinidad	79°	81°	J	F	M	A	M	**J**	**J**	**A**	**S**	O	N	D

Answer these questions on Extract A.

1 Explain the term 'archipelago' (line 4).

_____

2 Why do you think that different languages are spoken on different islands?

_____

_____

3 Explain how the location of the Caribbean islands is beneficial to their economies.

_____

_____

4 Which island would you visit if you were particularly interested in:

a festivals? _____   b history? _____

c adrenalin sports? _____

5 Which two-word term is used to describe a place that has a variety of natural flora and fauna?

_____

6 What type of source do you think Extract A has been taken from? Support your answer with SIX pieces of evidence.

B 2

_____

_____

_____

_____

_____

4

_____

Answer these questions on Extract B.

7 Look again at the phrase '…tips top ten…' (line 10)

B 2

a Which literary technique is this an example of? _____

b Find another example of where this technique is used in the text.

2

_____

8 It would be safer to eat a freshly prepared salad than a bowl of freshly cooked spicy vegetable stew. Do you agree with this statement? Use the text to support your answer.

B 2

_____

_____

2

_____

9 Explain why Caribbean islands with less tourism are likely to be safer than islands that experience higher levels of tourism. Use the text to support your answer.

B 2

_____

_____

_____

2

_____

Answer these questions on Extract C.

10 Is it possible to tour the nine Caribbean islands over 12 months and never experience a rainy season? Refer to the text in your answer.

B 2

_____

_____

2

_____

11 Which island experiences each of the following weather conditions?

B 2

a a non-fluctuating temperature _____

b the longest rainy season _____

c the widest range of temperature _____

3

Answer these questions on more than one extract.

12 Give an alternative for each word as it is used in the text.

B 2

a affluent (Extract B line 27) _____

b susceptible (Extract A line 24) _____

2

13 Tick the TWO statements that are true.

B 2

A The same fish can always be seen in the clear waters. ☐

B Creole is a new, popular language. ☐

C Grenada has a greater fluctuation in temperature range than Haiti. ☐

D The US Virgin Islands are a safe place to visit. ☐

E Infection can be exacerbated in a hot climate. ☐

2

14 Which word, as used in the text, means the same as each of these words?

B 2

a landscape (Extract A) _____

b victim (Extract B) _____

2

15 Why do you think that so many tourists visit the Caribbean islands each year? Support your answer with SEVEN pieces of evidence from the text.

B 2

_____

_____

_____

_____

_____

_____

_____

_____

7

Paper 4

By this time they were got to
the Enchanted Ground, where
the air naturally tended to make
one drowsy. And that place
was all grown over with briars
and thorns, excepting here and
there, where was an enchanted
arbor, upon which if a man sits,
or in which if a man sleeps, it is
a question, some say, whether
ever he shall rise or wake again
in this world. Over this forest,
therefore, they went, both one
and another, and Mr. Great-
Heart went before, for that he

was the guide; and Mr. Valiant-for-truth came behind, being rear-guard, for fear
lest peradventure some fiend, or dragon, or giant, or thief, should fall upon their
rear, and so do mischief. They went on here, each man with his sword drawn in his
hand; for they knew it was a dangerous place. Also they cheered up one another as
well as they could. Feeble-mind, Mr. Great-Heart commanded should come up after
him; and Mr. Despondency was under the eye of Mr. Valiant.

Now they had not gone far, but a great mist and darkness fell upon them all;
so that they could scarce, for a great while, the one see the other. Wherefore they
were forced, for some time, to feel one for another by words; for they walked not by
sight. But any one must think, that here was but sorry going for the best of them all;
but how much worse for the women and children, who both of feet and heart were
but tender! Yet so it was, that through the encouraging words of him that led in the
front, and of him that brought them up behind, they made a pretty good shift to wag
along.

The way also here was very wearisome, through dirt and slabbiness. Nor was
there, on all this ground, so much as one inn or victualling-house wherein to refresh
the feebler sort. Here, therefore, was grunting, and puffing, and sighing, while one
tumbleth over a bush, another sticks fast in the dirt, and the children, some of them,
lost their shoes in the mire; while one cries out, I am down; and another, Ho, where
are you? And a third, The bushes have got such fast hold on me; I think I cannot
get away from them.

Then they came at an arbor, warm, and promising much refreshing to the
pilgrims; for it was finely wrought above-head, beautified with greens, furnished with
benches and settles. It also had in it a soft couch, whereon the weary might lean.
This, you must think, all things considered, was tempting; for the pilgrims already
began to be foiled with the badness of the way: but there was not one of them
that made so much as a motion to stop there. Yea, for aught I could perceive, they
continually gave so good heed to the advice of their guide, and he did so faithfully
tell them of dangers, and of the nature of the dangers when they were at them, that
usually, when they were nearest to them, they did most pluck up their spirits, and
hearten one another to deny the flesh. This arbor was called The Slothful's Friend,

and was made on purpose to allure, if it might be, some of the pilgrims there to take up their rest when weary.

I saw them in my dream, that they went on in this their solitary ground, till they came to a place at which a man is apt to lose his way. Now, though when it was light their guide could well enough tell how to miss those ways that led wrong, yet in the dark he was put to a stand. But he had in his pocket a map of all ways leading to or from the Celestial City; wherefore he struck a light (for he never goes without his tinder-box also), and takes a view of his book or map, which bids him to be careful in that place to turn to the right hand. And had he not been careful here to look in his map, they had all, in probability, been smothered in the mud; for just a little before them, and that at the end of the cleanest way too, was a pit, none knows how deep, full of nothing but mud, there made on purpose to destroy the pilgrims in.

Then thought I with myself, Who that goeth on pilgrimage but would have one of these maps about him, that he may look, when he is at a stand, which is the way he must take?

Then they went on in this Enchanted Ground till they came to where there was another arbor, and it was built by the highway-side. And in that arbor there lay two men, whose names were Heedless and Too-bold. These two went thus far on pilgrimage; but here, being wearied with their journey, they sat down to rest themselves, and so fell fast asleep. When the pilgrims saw them, they stood still, and shook their heads; for they knew that the sleepers were in a pitiful case. Then they consulted what to do, whether to go on and leave them in their sleep, or to step to them and try to awake them; so they concluded to go to them and awake them, that is, if they could; but with this caution, namely, to take heed that they themselves did not sit down nor embrace the offered benefit of that arbor.

So they went in, and spake to the men, and called each by his name, for the guide, it seems, did know them; but there was no voice nor answer. Then the guide did shake them, and do what he could to disturb them. Then said one of them, I will pay you when I take my money. At which the guide shook his head. I will fight so long as I can hold my sword in my hand, said the other.

From *Pilgrim's Progress* by John Bunyan

1 What was the travellers' destination?

_____

2 How did the group of travellers first become aware of the fact that they were walking in a dangerous area?

_____

3 Describe, in your own words, the first arbor that the travellers passed.

_____

_____

_____

4 Why did the group choose not to rest at this first arbor? Refer to the text in your answer.

B 2

_____

_____

2

5 What does each phrase mean, in the context of the extract?

B 2

a '...to feel one for another by words...' (line 24)

_____

_____

b '...they made a pretty good shift to wag along...' (lines 28–29)

_____

_____

c '...embrace the offered benefit...' (line 72)

_____

_____

d '...for they walked not by sight...' (lines 24–25)

_____

4

_____

6 Explain, in your own words, what the travellers thought would happen to them if a careful watch wasn't kept at the back of the group.

B 2

_____

_____

2

_____

7 Find one word which, as used in the extract:

B 2

a means 'as a result' _____   **b** describes 'a journey' _____

2

8 What is interesting about the way in which the author displays the personality traits of several travellers? Support your answer with evidence from the text.

B 2

_____

_____

_____

2

_____

9 What is meant by each of these terms, as used in the text?

    a enchanted (line 7) _____   **b** lest (line 17) _____

    c foiled (line 41) _____   **d** allure (line 47) _____

10 Why were the pilgrims saddened to see some fellow travellers asleep?

_____

_____

_____

11 Describe, in your own words, how the group remained motivated during their journey. Use the text to support your answer.

_____

_____

_____

12 This extract has not been taken from a modern source. Find a word or short phrase in each section of text below to support this statement.

    a lines 42–45 _____   **b** lines 60–62 _____

    c lines 73–77 _____

13 The Enchanted Ground is a place for entrapment. Do you agree with this statement? Support your answer with SIX pieces of evidence.

_____

_____

_____

_____

_____

_____

_____

Now go to the Progress Chart to record your score!   Total 35

Paper 5

I visited Edinburgh with <u>languid</u> eyes and mind; and yet that city might have
interested the most unfortunate being. Clerval did not like it so well as Oxford,
for the <u>antiquity</u> of the latter city was more pleasing to him. But the beauty and
<u>regularity</u> of the new town of Edinburgh, its romantic castle and its <u>environs</u>, the
<u>most delightful</u> in the world, Arthur's Seat, St. Bernard's Well, and the Pentland Hills   5
compensated him for the change and filled him with cheerfulness and admiration.
But I was impatient to arrive at the <u>termination</u> of my journey.

 We left Edinburgh in a week, passing through Coupar, St. Andrew's, and along
the banks of the Tay, to Perth, where our friend expected us. But I was in no mood
to laugh and talk with strangers or enter into their feelings or plans with the good   10
humour expected from a guest; and accordingly I told Clerval that I wished to make
the tour of Scotland alone. "Do you," said I, "enjoy yourself, and let this be our
rendezvous. I may be absent a month or two; but do not interfere with my motions,
I entreat you; leave me to peace and solitude for a short time; and when I return, I
hope it will be with a lighter heart, more congenial to your own temper."   15

 Henry wished to dissuade me, but seeing me bent on this plan, ceased to
remonstrate. He entreated me to write often. "I had rather be with you," he said, "in
your solitary rambles, than with these Scotch people, whom I do not know; hasten,
then, my dear friend, to return, that I may again feel myself somewhat at home,
which I cannot do in your absence."   20

 Having parted from my friend, I determined to visit some remote spot of Scotland,
and finish my work in solitude. I did not doubt but that the monster followed me,
and would discover himself to me when I should have finished, that he might
receive his companion. With this resolution I traversed the northern highlands, and
fixed on one of the remotest of the Orkneys as the scene of my labours. It was a   25
place fitted for such a work, being hardly more than a rock, whose high sides were
continually beaten upon by the waves. The soil was barren, scarcely affording
pasture for a few miserable cows, and oatmeal for its inhabitants, which consisted
of five persons, whose gaunt and scraggy limbs gave tokens of their miserable fare.
Vegetables and bread, when they indulged in such luxuries, and even fresh water,   30
was to be procured from the main land, which was about five miles distant.

 On the whole island there were but three miserable huts, and one of these
was vacant when I arrived. This I hired. It contained but two rooms, and these
exhibited all the squalidness of the most miserable penury. The thatch had fallen

in, the walls were unplastered, and the door was off its hinges. I ordered it to be   35
repaired, bought some furniture, and took possession; an incident which would,
doubtless, have occasioned some surprise, had not all the senses of the cottagers
been benumbed by want and squalid poverty. As it was, I lived ungazed at and
unmolested, hardly thanked for the pittance of food and clothes which I gave; so
much does suffering blunt even the coarsest sensations of men.   40

In this retreat I devoted the morning to labour; but in the evening, when the
weather permitted, I walked on the stony beach of the sea, to listen to the waves
as they roared and dashed at my feet. It was a monotonous yet ever-changing
scene. I thought of Switzerland; it was far different from this desolate and appalling
landscape. Its hills are covered with vines, and its cottages are scattered thickly   45
in the plains. Its fair lakes reflect a blue and gentle sky; and, when troubled by
the winds, their tumult is but as the play of a lively infant, when compared to the
roarings of the giant ocean.

In this manner I distributed my occupations when I first arrived, but as I
proceeded in my labour, it became every day more horrible and irksome to me.   50
Sometimes I could not prevail on myself to enter my laboratory for several days,
and at other times I toiled day and night in order to complete my work. It was,
indeed, a filthy process in which I was engaged. During my first experiment, a kind
of enthusiastic frenzy had blinded me to the horror of my employment; my mind
was intently fixed on the consummation of my labour, and my eyes were shut to the   55
horror of my proceedings. But now I went to it in cold blood, and my heart often
sickened at the work of my hands.

Thus situated, employed in the most detestable occupation, immersed in a
solitude where nothing could for an instant call my attention from the actual scene
in which I was engaged, my spirits became unequal; I grew restless and nervous.   60
Every moment I feared to meet my persecutor. Sometimes I sat with my eyes
fixed on the ground, fearing to raise them lest they should encounter the object
which I so much dreaded to behold. I feared to wander from the sight of my fellow
creatures lest when alone he should come to claim his companion.

In the mean time I worked on, and my labour was already considerably   65
advanced. I looked towards its completion with a tremulous and eager hope,
which I dared not trust myself to question but which was intermixed with obscure
forebodings of evil that made my heart sicken in my bosom.

From *Frankenstein* by Mary Shelley

1 Explain why Clerval preferred Oxford to Edinburgh.   B 2

_____   1

2 Approximately how many weeks would Clerval have to remain in Perth?   B 2

_____   1

3 What is meant by the phrase, '...visited Edinburgh with languid eyes and
 mind...'? (line 1)   B 2

_____

_____   2

4 Give TWO reasons why the **narrator** goes to the island.

_____

_____

5 What does each phrase mean, in the context of the extract?

   a '…more congenial to your own temper…' (line 15)

_____

_____

   b '…whose gaunt and scraggy limbs gave tokens of their miserable fare…' (line 29)

_____

_____

   c '…my spirits became unequal…' (line 60)

_____

_____

6 What was the staple food in the island inhabitants' diet?

_____

7 Give an alternative for each of these words, as used in the context of the extract.

   a remote (line 21) _____   **b** irksome (line 50) _____

   c traversed (line 24) _____

8 Tick the TWO statements that are false.

   A The **narrator** begged his companion to leave him alone. ☐

   B The roof of the **narrator's** hut was in a state of good repair. ☐

   C The Orkneys are in the far north of Scotland. ☐

   D The **narrator** worked every day to complete his awful task. ☐

   E The Tay is a Scottish river. ☐

9 Which word, as used in the extract, means the same as each of these terms?

   a surroundings _____   **b** food _____

   c obtained _____

10 What type of occupation do you think the **narrator** holds? Support your answer with TWO pieces of evidence from the text.

_____

_____

_____

3

11 Describe the difference between the **narrator's** attitude during his initial investigations and his later work. Refer to the text in your answer.

_____

_____

_____

_____

4

12 How does the **narrator** make Switzerland sound like a more inviting place than the island? Support your answer with TEN pieces of evidence from the text.

_____

_____

_____

_____

_____

_____

_____

_____

_____

_____

_____

_____

10

ACT I. SCENE 1.
London. A street
[Enter RICHARD, DUKE OF GLOUCESTER]
GLOUCESTER: Now is the winter of our discontent
   Made glorious summer by this sun of York;
   And all the clouds that lour'd upon our house   5
   In the deep bosom of the ocean buried.
   Now are our brows bound with victorious wreaths;
   Our bruised arms hung up for monuments;
   Our stern alarums chang'd to merry meetings,
   Our dreadful marches to delightful measures.   10
   Grim-visag'd war hath smooth'd his wrinkled front,
   And now, instead of mounting barbed steeds
   To fright the souls of fearful adversaries,
   He capers nimbly in a lady's chamber
   To the lascivious pleasing of a lute.   15
   But I – that am not shap'd for sportive tricks,
   Nor made to court an amorous looking-glass –
   I – that am rudely stamp'd, and want love's majesty
   To strut before a wanton ambling nymph –
   I – that am curtail'd of this fair proportion,   20
   Cheated of feature by dissembling nature,
   Deform'd, unfinish'd, sent before my time
   Into this breathing world scarce half made up,
   And that so lamely and unfashionable
   That dogs bark at me as I halt by them –   25
   Why, I, in this weak piping time of peace,
   Have no delight to pass away the time,
   Unless to spy my shadow in the sun
   And descant on mine own deformity.
   And therefore, since I cannot prove a lover   30
   To entertain these fair well-spoken days,
   I am determined to prove a villain
   And hate the idle pleasures of these days.
   Plots have I laid, inductions dangerous,
   By drunken prophecies, libels, and dreams,   35
   To set my brother Clarence and the King
   In deadly hate the one against the other;
   And if King Edward be as true and just
   As I am subtle, false, and treacherous,
   This day should Clarence closely be mew'd up –   40
   About a prophecy which says that G
   Of Edward's heirs the murderer shall be.
   Dive, thoughts, down to my soul. Here Clarence comes.

[Enter CLARENCE, guarded, and BRAKENBURY]
   Brother, good day. What means this armed guard   45

That waits upon your Grace?

CLARENCE: His Majesty,
    Tend'ring my person's safety, hath appointed
    This conduct to convey me to th' Tower.

GLOUCESTER: Upon what cause?   50

CLARENCE: Because my name is George.

GLOUCESTER: Alack, my lord, that fault is none of yours:
    He should, for that, commit your godfathers.
    O, belike his Majesty hath some intent
    That you should be new-christ'ned in the Tower.   55
    But what's the matter, Clarence? May I know?

CLARENCE: Yea, Richard, when I know; for I protest
    As yet I do not; but, as I can learn,
    He hearkens after prophecies and dreams,
    And from the cross-row plucks the letter G,   60
    And says a wizard told him that by G
    His issue disinherited should be;
    And, for my name of George begins with G,
    It follows in his thought that I am he.
    These, as I learn, and such like toys as these   65
    Hath mov'd his Highness to commit me now.

GLOUCESTER: Why, this it is when men are rul'd by women:
    'Tis not the King that sends you to the Tower;
    My Lady Grey his wife, Clarence, 'tis she
    That tempers him to this extremity.   70
    Was it not she and that good man of worship,
    Antony Woodville, her brother there,
    That made him send Lord Hastings to the Tower,
    From whence this present day he is delivered?
    We are not safe, Clarence; we are not safe.   75

CLARENCE: By heaven, I think there is no man is secure
    But the Queen's kindred, and night-walking heralds
    That trudge betwixt the King and Mistress Shore.
    Heard you not what an humble suppliant
    Lord Hastings was, for her delivery?   80

GLOUCESTER: Humbly complaining to her deity
    Got my Lord Chamberlain his liberty.
    I'll tell you what – I think it is our way,
    If we will keep in favour with the King,
    To be her men and wear her livery: 85
    The jealous o'er-worn widow, and herself,
    Since that our brother dubb'd them gentlewomen,
    Are mighty gossips in our monarchy.

BRAKENBURY: I beseech your Graces both to pardon me:
    His Majesty hath straitly given in charge   90
    That no man shall have private conference,
    Of what degree soever, with your brother.

GLOUCESTER: Even so; an't please your worship, Brakenbury,
    You may partake of any thing we say:
    We speak no treason, man; we say the King   95

Is wise and virtuous, and his noble queen
Well struck in years, fair, and not jealous;
We say that Shore's wife hath a pretty foot,
A cherry lip, a bonny eye, a passing pleasing tongue;
And that the Queen's kindred are made gentlefolks.   100
How say you, sir? Can you deny all this?
BRAKENBURY: With this, my lord, myself have naught to do.
GLOUCESTER: Naught to do with Mistress Shore! I tell thee, fellow,
    He that doth naught with her, excepting one,
    Were best to do it secretly alone.   105
BRAKENBURY: What one, my lord?
GLOUCESTER: Her husband, knave! Wouldst thou betray me?
BRAKENBURY: I do beseech your Grace to pardon me, and withal
    Forbear your conference with the noble Duke.
CLARENCE: We know thy charge, Brakenbury, and will obey.   110
GLOUCESTER: We are the Queen's abjects and must obey.
    Brother, farewell; I will unto the King;
    And whatsoe'er you will employ me in –
    Were it to call King Edward's widow sister –
    I will perform it to enfranchise you.   115
    Meantime, this deep disgrace in brotherhood
    Touches me deeper than you can imagine.
CLARENCE: I know it pleaseth neither of us well.
GLOUCESTER: Well, your imprisonment shall not be long;
    I will deliver or else lie for you.   120
    Meantime, have patience.
CLARENCE: I must perforce. Farewell.
[Exeunt CLARENCE, BRAKENBURY, and guard]
GLOUCESTER: Go tread the path that thou shalt ne'er return.
    Simple, plain Clarence, I do love thee so   125
    That I will shortly send thy soul to heaven,
    If heaven will take the present at our hands.

From *Richard III* by William Shakespeare

Answer these questions.

1 Which one-word term can be used to describe Gloucester's opening speech?

B 2

1

_____

2 Reread the first 15 lines. Find THREE pieces of evidence that show that the
   recent battles are now over.

B 2

_____

_____

_____

3

_____

3 Explain why Gloucester decides to develop a wicked nature.

_____

_____

_____

_____

4 What is Gloucester's goal?

_____

_____

5 Why has the King issued an order for Clarence to be sent to the Tower?

_____

_____

6 In what TWO ways does Gloucester try to explain the King's actions against Clarence? Refer to the text in your answer.

_____

_____

7 Explain, in your own words, what each phrase means as used in the extract.

  a '…To be her men and wear her livery…' (line 85)

_____

_____

  b '…That no man shall have private conference…' (line 91)

_____

_____

8 In which THREE ways does Gloucester refer to the Queen?

_____

9 Write a character description of Clarence. Refer to the text in your answer.

_____

_____

_____

10 Give an alternative for each word as it is used in the text.

B 2

a beseech (line 89) _____   **b** bonny (line 99) _____

c enfranchise (line 115) _____

3

11 '...Clarence, I do love thee so...' (line 125) Do you think Gloucester means this? Support your answer with reference to the text.

B 2

_____

_____

_____

_____

2

12 Gloucester is a physically attractive man. Do you agree with this statement? Support your answer with FIVE pieces of evidence from the text.

B 2

_____

_____

_____

_____

_____

_____

5

13 This extract has been taken from a playscript. Find FIVE pieces of evidence to support this statement.

B 1

_____

_____

_____

_____

_____

_____

5

Paper 7

Part I

On either side the river lie
Long fields of barley and of rye,
That clothe the wold and meet the sky;
And thro' the field the road runs by
To many-tower'd Camelot;   5
And up and down the people go,
Gazing where the lilies blow
Round an island there below,
The island of Shalott.

Willows whiten, aspens quiver,   10
Little breezes dusk and shiver
Thro' the wave that runs for ever
By the island in the river
Flowing down to Camelot.
Four gray walls, and four gray towers,   15
Overlook a space of flowers,
And the silent isle imbowers
The Lady of Shalott.

By the margin, willow veil'd,
Slide the heavy barges trail'd   20
By slow horses; and unhail'd
The shallop flitteth silken-sail'd
Skimming down to Camelot:
But who hath seen her wave her hand?
Or at the casement seen her stand?   25
Or is she known in all the land,
The Lady of Shalott?

Only reapers, reaping early
In among the bearded barley,
Hear a song that echoes cheerly   30
From the river winding clearly,
Down to tower'd Camelot:
And by the moon the reaper weary,
Piling sheaves in uplands airy,
Listening, whispers "'Tis the fairy   35
Lady of Shalott."

Part II

There she weaves by night and day
A magic web with colours gay.
She has heard a whisper say,
A curse is on her if she stay   40
To look down to Camelot.
She knows not what the curse may be,
And so she weaveth steadily,
And little other care hath she,
The Lady of Shalott.   45

And moving thro' a mirror clear
That hangs before her all the year,
Shadows of the world appear.
There she sees the highway near
Winding down to Camelot: 50
There the river eddy whirls,
And there the surly village-churls,
And the red cloaks of market girls,
Pass onward from Shalott.

Sometimes a troop of damsels glad,   55
An abbot on an ambling pad,
Sometimes a curly shepherd-lad,
Or long-hair'd page in crimson clad,
Goes by to tower'd Camelot;
And sometimes thro' the mirror blue   60
The knights come riding two and two:
She hath no loyal knight and true,
The Lady of Shalott.

But in her web she still delights
To weave the mirror's magic sights,   65
For often thro' the silent nights
A funeral, with plumes and lights
And music, went to Camelot:
Or when the moon was overhead,
Came two young lovers lately wed: 70
"I am half sick of shadows," said
The Lady of Shalott.

Part III

A bow-shot from her bower-eaves,
He rode between the barley-sheaves,
The sun came dazzling thro' the leaves, 75
And flamed upon the brazen greaves
Of bold Sir Lancelot.
A red-cross knight for ever kneel'd
To a lady in his shield,
That sparkled on the yellow field, 80
Beside remote Shalott.

The gemmy bridle glitter'd free,
Like to some branch of stars we see
Hung in the golden Galaxy.
The bridle bells rang merrily 85
As he rode down to Camelot:
And from his blazon'd baldric slung
A mighty silver bugle hung,
And as he rode his armour rung,
Beside remote Shalott. 90

All in the blue unclouded weather
Thick-jewell'd shone the saddle-leather,
The helmet and the helmet-feather
Burn'd like one burning flame together,
As he rode down to Camelot. 95
As often thro' the purple night,
Below the starry clusters bright,
Some bearded meteor, trailing light,
Moves over still Shalott.

His broad clear brow in sunlight glow'd; 100
On burnish'd hooves his war-horse trode;
From underneath his helmet flow'd
His coal-black curls as on he rode,
As he rode down to Camelot.
From the bank and from the river 105
He flash'd into the crystal mirror,
"Tirra lirra," by the river
Sang Sir Lancelot.

She left the web, she left the loom,
She made three paces thro' the room, 110
She saw the water-lily bloom,
She saw the helmet and the plume,
She look'd down to Camelot.
Out flew the web and floated wide;
The mirror crack'd from side to side; 115
"The curse is come upon me," cried
The Lady of Shalott.

Part IV

In the stormy east-wind straining,
The pale yellow woods were waning,
The broad stream in his banks complaining, *120*
Heavily the low sky raining
Over tower'd Camelot;
Down she came and found a boat
Beneath a willow left afloat, *125*
And round about the prow she wrote
The Lady of Shalott.

And down the river's dim expanse
Like some bold seer in a trance,
Seeing all his own mischance – *130*
With a glassy countenance
Did she look to Camelot.
And at the closing of the day
She loosed the chain, and down she lay;
The broad stream bore her far away, *135*
The Lady of Shalott.

Lying, robed in snowy white
That loosely flew to left and right –
The leaves upon her falling light –
Thro' the noises of the night *140*
She floated down to Camelot:
And as the boat-head wound along
The willowy hills and fields among,
They heard her singing her last song,
The Lady of Shalott. *145*

Heard a carol, mournful, holy,
Chanted loudly, chanted lowly,
Till her blood was frozen slowly,
And her eyes were darken'd wholly,
Turn'd to tower'd Camelot. *150*
For ere she reach'd upon the tide
The first house by the water-side,
Singing in her song she died,
The Lady of Shalott.

Under tower and balcony, *155*
By garden-wall and gallery,
A gleaming shape she floated by,
Dead-pale between the houses high,
Silent into Camelot.
Out upon the wharfs they came, *160*
Knight and burgher, lord and dame,
And round the prow they read her name,
The Lady of Shalott.

Who is this? and what is here?
And in the lighted palace near *165*
Died the sound of royal cheer;
And they cross'd themselves for fear,
All the knights at Camelot:
But Lancelot mused a little space;
He said, "She has a lovely face; *170*
God in his mercy lend her grace,
The Lady of Shalott."

The Lady of Shalott by Alfred Lord Tennyson

Answer these questions on Part I.

1 Where does the Lady live?

B 2

2

_____

2 The people of Camelot see the Lady as they go about their business. Do you
   agree with this statement? Refer to THREE pieces of evidence in your answer.

B 2

_____

_____

_____

3

Answer these questions on Part II.

3 Reread verses 5–6 and then answer these questions.

B 2

   a How does the Lady see the world?

_____

1

   b Explain why she uses this method. Refer to the text in your answer.

_____

_____

2

4 How does the Lady occupy herself each day?

B 2

_____

2

5 Reread lines 37–70. At this point in the poem, do you think the Lady is happy?
   Explain your answer with reference to the text.

B 2

_____

_____

2

Answer these questions on Part III.

6 What do we learn about Lancelot in this section? Support your answer with
   FOUR pieces of evidence from the text.

B 2

_____

_____

_____

_____

4

7 Describe TWO ways in which the poet shows that Sir Lancelot is an important character in the poem.

_____

_____

_____

_____

B 2

2

Answer these questions on Part IV.

8 Why did the Lady make her journey in Part IV? Find TWO pieces of text from anywhere in the poem to support your answer.

_____

_____

_____

B 2

2

9 Does the Lady achieve her goal? Explain your answer with reference to the text.

_____

_____

_____

B 2

2

10 How do the people of Camelot learn the identity of the Lady?

_____

B 2

1

11 Upon seeing the Lady, explain how Sir Lancelot's reaction is different to that of the other knights.

_____

_____

B 2

2

12 What does each phrase mean, as used in the poem?

a '…woods were waning…' (line 119)

_____

b '…with a glassy countenance…' (line 131)

_____

B 2

2

33

Answer these questions, which relate to more than one Part.

13 Give an alternative for each of these words as they are used in the context of the extract.

a plume (line 112) _____   b seer (line 129) _____

c wholly (line 149) _____   d imbowers (line 17) _____

14 Find an example of each of the following literary techniques.

a **alliteration** (in Part I) _____

b a **simile** (in Part III) _____

15 Tick the TWO statements that are true.

A The Lady began her journey early in the morning. ☐

B The Lady was a fairy. ☐

C There are sheep in, or near to, Camelot. ☐

D Boats full of cargo are pulled along the river. ☐

E The knight and burgher hear the Lady singing. ☐

Now go to the Progress Chart to record your score!   Total 35

Paper 8

Extracted from a Family Paper

I

I address these lines – written in India – to my relatives in England.

My object is to explain the motive which has induced me to refuse the right hand of friendship to my cousin, John Herncastle. The reserve which I have hitherto maintained in this matter has been misinterpreted by members of my family whose good opinion I cannot consent to forfeit. I request them to suspend their decision until they have read my narrative. And I declare, on my word of honour, that what I am now about to write is, strictly and literally, the truth.

The private difference between my cousin and me took its rise in a great public event in which we were both concerned – the storming of Seringapatam, under General Baird, on the 4th of May, 1799.

In order that the circumstances may be clearly understood, I must revert for a moment to the period before the assault, and to the stories current in our camp of the treasure in jewels and gold stored up in the Palace of Seringapatam.

II

One of the wildest of these stories related to a Yellow Diamond – a famous gem in the native annals of India.

The earliest known traditions describe the stone as having been set in the forehead of the four-handed Indian god who typifies the Moon. Partly from its peculiar colour, partly from a superstition which represented it as feeling the influence of the deity whom it adorned, and growing and lessening in lustre with the waxing and waning of the moon, it first gained the name by which it continues to be known in India to this day – the name of THE MOONSTONE. A similar superstition was once prevalent, as I have heard, in ancient Greece and Rome; not applying, however (as in India), to a diamond devoted to the service of a god, but to a semi-transparent stone of the inferior order of gems, supposed to be affected by the lunar influences – the moon, in this latter case also, giving the name by which the stone is still known to collectors in our own time. The adventures of the Yellow Diamond begin with the eleventh century of the Christian era. At that date, the Mohammedan conqueror, Mahmoud of Ghizni, crossed India; seized on the holy city of Somnauth; and stripped of its treasures the famous temple, which had stood for centuries – the shrine of Hindoo pilgrimage, and the wonder of the Eastern world.

Of all the deities worshipped in the temple, the moon-god alone escaped the rapacity of the conquering Mohammedans. Preserved by three Brahmins, the inviolate deity, bearing the Yellow Diamond in its forehead, was removed by night,

5

10

15

20

25

30

35

40

and was transported to the second of the sacred cities of India – the city of Benares.

Here, in a new shrine – in a hall inlaid with precious stones, under a roof supported by pillars of gold – the moon-god was set up and worshipped. Here, on the night when the shrine was completed, Vishnu the Preserver appeared to the three Brahmins in a dream.

The deity breathed the breath of his divinity on the Diamond in the forehead of the god. And the Brahmins knelt and hid their faces in their robes. The deity commanded that the Moonstone should be watched, from that time forth, by three priests in turn, night and day, to the end of the generations of men. And the Brahmins heard, and bowed before his will. The deity predicted certain disaster to the presumptuous mortal who laid hands on the sacred gem, and to all of his house and name who received it after him. And the Brahmins caused the prophecy to be written over the gates of the shrine in letters of gold.

One age followed another – and still, generation after generation, the successors of the three Brahmins watched their priceless Moonstone, night and day. One age followed another until the first years of the eighteenth Christian century saw the reign of Aurungzebe, Emperor of the Moguls. At his command havoc and rapine were let loose once more among the temples of the worship of Brahmah. The shrine of the four-handed god was polluted by the slaughter of sacred animals; the images of the deities were broken in pieces; and the Moonstone was seized by an officer of rank in the army of Aurungzebe.

Powerless to recover their lost treasure by open force, the three guardian priests followed and watched it in disguise. The generations succeeded each other; the warrior who had committed the sacrilege perished miserably; the Moonstone passed (carrying its curse with it) from one lawless Mohammedan hand to another; and still, through all chances and changes, the successors of the three guardian priests kept their watch, waiting the day when the will of Vishnu the Preserver should restore to them their sacred gem. Time rolled on from the first to the last years of the eighteenth Christian century. The Diamond fell into the possession of Tippoo, Sultan of Seringapatam, who caused it to be placed as an ornament in the handle of a dagger, and who commanded it to be kept among the choicest treasures of his armoury. Even then – in the palace of the Sultan himself – the three guardian priests still kept their watch in secret. There were three officers of Tippoo's household, strangers to the rest, who had won their master's confidence by conforming, or appearing to conform, to the Mussulman faith; and to those three men report pointed as the three priests in disguise.

III

So, as told in our camp, ran the fanciful story of the Moonstone. It made no serious impression on any of us except my cousin – whose love of the marvellous induced him to believe it. On the night before the assault on Seringapatam, he was absurdly angry with me, and with others, for treating the whole thing as a fable. A foolish wrangle followed; and Herncastle's unlucky temper got the better of him. He declared, in his boastful way, that we should see the Diamond on his finger, if the English army took Seringapatam. The sally was saluted by a roar of laughter, and there, as we all thought that night, the thing ended.

Let me now take you on to the day of the assault. My cousin and I were separated at the outset. I never saw him when we forded the river; when we planted the English flag in the first breach; when we crossed the ditch beyond; and, fighting

every inch of our way, entered the town. It was only at dusk, when the place was *90*
ours, and after General Baird himself had found the dead body of Tippoo under a
heap of the slain, that Herncastle and I met.

We were each attached to a party sent out by the general's orders to prevent the
plunder and confusion which followed our conquest. The camp-followers committed
deplorable excesses; and, worse still, the soldiers found their way, by a guarded *95*
door, into the treasury of the Palace, and loaded themselves with gold and jewels. It
was in the court outside the treasury that my cousin and I met, to enforce the laws
of discipline on our own soldiers. Herncastle's fiery temper had been, as I could
plainly see, exasperated to a kind of frenzy by the terrible slaughter through which
we had passed. He was very unfit, in my opinion, to perform the duty that had been *100*
entrusted to him.

From *The Moonstone* by Wilkie Collins

Answer these questions.

1 What do you understand the **verb** 'to storm' to mean, in the context of this extract?

_____

2 What occupation do you think the **narrator** holds? Explain your answer.

_____

_____

3 Explain what has prompted the **narrator** to write this account.

_____

_____

4 Explain why the gem was called 'The Moonstone'. Support your answer with THREE pieces of evidence.

_____

_____

_____

_____

5 Explain why the stone was not destroyed in the attack on Somnauth.

_____

_____

_____

6 Explain, in your own words, the prediction that was foretold about the stone.

_____

_____

_____

_____

7 At what point does the reader first learn that there was some truth to the prediction?

_____

8 Explain why the three Brahmins did not take the stone back after it was seized in the 18th century.

_____

9 When did the Brahmins think they would get the stone back?

_____

10 Which **adjective** shows that the **narrator** did not believe in the tale of the stone?

_____

11 Why was the **narrator** sent out with a group of men after the British victory?

_____

_____

_____

12 Which other term is used for each of these words in the context of the extract?

a 'god' _____ **b** 'moon' _____

13 Tick the TWO statements that are true.

A Mahmoud of Ghizni added the gem to his dagger. ☐

B At some point, Tippoo owned the Moonstone. ☐

C The **narrator** is writing this account for his private diary. ☐

D The writer viewed his cousin as a friend. ☐

E When Vishnu appeared to them, the Brahmins averted their eyes. ☐

14 Give an alternative for each word as it is used in the text.   B 2

    a prevalent (line 30) _____   **b** rapacity (line 40) _____

    c deplorable (line 95) _____   **d** wrangle (line 83) _____   4

15 Underline one word that best describes: B 2

    a Benares: luminous   fortified   consecrated   rich

    b Vishnu: omnipotent   protector   vindictive   angry

    c Aurungzebe: officer   general   sultan   sovereign   3

16 How would you describe John Herncastle's character? Explain your answer with reference to the text.   B 2

_____

_____

_____

_____   3

17 Do you think this extract comes from a work of fiction or fact? Support your answer with evidence from the text.   B 1

_____

_____

_____

_____   2

Now go to the Progress Chart to record your score!   **Total**   35

Paper 9

Would you like to fly in my beautiful balloon?
The hot air balloon is the oldest form of human flight, with the first person up in
the air on 21 November 1783 in Paris, France. The balloon was created by the
Montgolfier Brothers. A hot air balloon is made quite simply with a balloon (the
envelope) that contains heated air and a basket or gondola underneath to carry the   5
passengers and the source of heat. Because the heated air inside the envelope has
a lower density than the colder air outside of the envelope, the balloon becomes
buoyant. The burner, which is connected to the basket, injects a flame into the
envelope and it is commonly fuelled by a liquefied gas, such as propane, which is
stored in pressurised containers.   10

Click here to see pictures of the Montgolfier Brothers   **HOME**

The envelopes in modern hot air balloons are frequently made out of strong,
lightweight material such as polyester or rip-strong nylon. To make an envelope the
material is cut into shaped panels and is then sewn along with load tapes, which
are structural devices that help to carry the weight of the basket and passengers.
There can be anything from 4 to over 24 panels in an envelope. The tops of the   15
panels are attached to a hoop of smooth aluminium, which holds the vertical
load tapes in place. Part of the fabric is often coated with silicon or polyurethane,
which acts as a sealer to ensure that air does not permeate. When this coating
degrades, it is the end of the road for the envelope because if it becomes porous,
it is effectively useless although there are products on the market today that can be   20
used to recoat the fabric giving an envelope a new lease of life.

There is a huge difference in the envelope sizes available. For a single passenger
in a tiny balloon the volume of the envelope sphere would be just under 600 m cubed
whereas the huge, commercial sightseeing hot air balloons can have an envelope
volume of nearly 17,000 m cubed and can carry 25 passengers or more! The shape   25
of the envelope can vary from the inverted teardrop, the most common shape, to
the specialised balloons designed for competitions – these are modified to minimise
aerodynamic drag. Likewise, the baskets range from little triangular spaces to large,
compartmentalised rectangles. The baskets usually have some form of foothold to
aid passengers getting in and out of the baskets. The baskets can be made of rattan,   30
wicker or aluminium, which is known for its lightweight qualities.

Click here to see hot air balloons in construction   **HOME**

To guide the vehicle, the envelope has a vent which can be opened to aid descent.
The size of the vent opening determines the speed with which the balloon will drop
but there are a whole range of instruments to help the pilot. An altimeter, a vertical
speed indicator and a range of temperature gauges are common and a GPS   35
receiver is invaluable for determining ground speed. If the pilot wants the balloon
lifted upwards, the air temperature inside the envelope needs to be raised and the
internal temperature can be anything up to 120˚C. If this temperature is maintained,

the envelope fabric can last for perhaps 500 hours of flying time before it needs replacing but to increase longevity, many pilots operate at lower temperatures.   40

The first Atlantic crossing in a balloon took place in 1978 through the use of Helium, but in 1987 Richard Branson crossed the Atlantic using a traditional burner and hot air. In 1981, the first Pacific crossing was made.

If you would like to own a hot air balloon, the largest manufacturer in the world is based in the UK and both Cameron and Lindstrand have staff available who will   45
help you choose the best balloon for you. You will of course need a licence to fly one. This can be gained via the Civil Aviation Authority and is specifically for hot air balloon pilots. Follow the links below for further information.

Click here for contact details of manufacturers

Click here to go to the CAA

HOME

Of course, safety is of prime importance in hot air ballooning. If the pilot light should go out, a flint spark lighter is vital and has saved many lives. The pilot must also   50
maintain the envelope, ensuring that it is stored clean and dry to inhibit mould. The basket must remain in tip-top condition, especially the anti-skid bottom that makes for a safe landing. The pilot must wear clothing of natural fibres as they do not melt and fire resistant gloves are critical in case of flame problems. The fuel container must be well maintained and many pilots carry a spare so that a safe landing could   55
be made should a blockage or fuel leak happen. The pilot and passengers should wear stout shoes and a helmet and should take every precaution to remain safe. That said, hot air ballooning is considered a very safe sport, as long as you are flying with a properly accredited pilot.

If you want to experience the high life, hundreds of trips every year are organised   60
by large commercial companies, as well as smaller balloonists, and they range in price depending upon the length of journey and where you will be flying. It is certainly worth a quick surf on the internet to find your nearest location. The main flying season is March to October, although winter flights can be beautiful. During the main season, flights are usually early morning or evening, as this is when the   65
wind is calmest and so provides a smooth, controlled ride.

If you aren't feeling brave enough for a trip but would love to see these majestic machines, there are hot air balloon events every month of the flying year. For example, the international balloon festival in Bristol every August is a sight to behold with balloonists travelling to it from all over the world. Watching the myriad   70
of colours and shapes grow before your eyes and then watching them all take off like a flock of parrots, rising gently and with the dignity that no other flying machine could ever possess, is an amazing experience. Perhaps more than with any other invention, the sight of a hot air balloon drifting calmly through our skies induces the awe and wonder that allows us to marvel at how anyone could have the vision to   75
devise such a creation.

Click here to see pictures of hot air balloons in flight

HOME

1 Explain how a hot air balloon rises. Refer to the text in your answer.

B 2

_____

_____

_____

_____

◯ 3

2 Why is propane an ideal gas for fuelling balloons?

B 2

_____

_____

_____

◯ 3

3 Why are top hoops made out of aluminium? Use the text to support your answer.

B 2

_____

_____

_____

◯ 2

4 Explain, in your own words, the role of the vent.

B 2

_____

_____

_____

_____

◯ 3

5 For how many years had the balloon existed before an Atlantic crossing was made using long-established methods?

B 2

_____

◯ 1

6 Tick the TWO statements that are true.

B 2

A With the temperature at 120°C a pilot could, in theory, fly continuously for one month. ☐

B Load tapes must be coated in silicon or polyurethane. ☐

C A fuel obstruction could be fatal. ☐

D Montgolfier flew the first hot air balloon. ☐

E Large baskets can have internal dividers. ☐

F The Civil Aviation Agency issues hot air ballooning certificates. ☐

◯ 2

7 Explain each of the following phrases, as it is used in the text.

    a '…becomes buoyant…' (lines 7–8)

    _____

    b '…does not permeate…' (line 18)

    _____

    c '…myriad of colours…' (lines 70–71)

    _____

    d '…to increase longevity…' (line 40)

    _____

8 Explain, in your own words, how competitive balloons are different.

_____

_____

_____

9 Give an alternative for each of these words, as used in the context of the extract.

    a accredited (line 59) _____   **b** inhibit (line 51) _____

    c devise (line 76) _____

10 Find an example of each of these literary techniques in the text.

    a a **simile** _____

    b **alliteration** _____

    c **personification** _____

11 Would it be advisable for a pilot to wear blue cotton trousers, a white wool pullover and black, sturdy leather shoes when flying? Refer to the text in your answer.

_____

_____

_____

B 2
B 2
4
B 2
2
B 2
3
B 2
3
B 2
2

12 To have a peaceful lunch flying above fields and villages, on a warm, sunny, August day would be perfect. Do you agree with this statement? Refer to the text in your answer.

B 2

_____

_____

_____

2

13 What type of source do you think this extract has been taken from? Support your answer with FOUR pieces of evidence.

B 1

_____

_____

_____

_____

_____

5

Now go to the Progress Chart to record your score!   Total   35

Paper 10

The famous Navigation Act, which brought on the war between England and Holland, was one of the last acts in the life of the great Englishman Oliver Cromwell. Before telling the stories of the fine old Sea Admirals who fought in that war for the power of the seas, let us see what this man Cromwell had already done for his country.

Oliver Cromwell was a very giant among men, the 'wonder of Europe and the glory of his age'. Like the Pilgrim Fathers, he was a Puritan, steeped in the language of his Bible, intolerant of Roman Catholics. He had a mighty brain and a great soul; but he was no perfect hero, no spotless saint. He was just a strong man, who did what he thought best for his country in a difficult age.

The young Oliver was four years old when Queen Elizabeth died and James became King of England. There is a story that, when he was a small baby, a large monkey seized him out of his cradle and carried him up on to the roof of the house. Another story says, that the very year of James's accession, his little son, Prince Charles, was worsted at 'fisticuffs' while playing with Oliver Cromwell, who was but a year older than himself. But as the little Prince did not speak till he was five, and crawled on his hands and knees till he was seven, this is not likely.

It was a sorry day for England when this same young prince became king, on the death of his father in 1625, and the long quarrels were begun which ended only with his execution.

Now, England was governed by a king and Parliament. This latter consisted of a number of men from all parts of the country who decided on laws and taxes for the good of the land. In this Parliament sat young Oliver Cromwell. No one thought much of him. He slouched in and out in a home-spun suit, took little part publicly, and seemed glad enough to return to his farm, his wife and children, near Ely, in the eastern counties. It was not till Charles had plunged his country into civil war, by reason of his unjust taxation, that Cromwell rose to play his great part.

There was no standing army in England at this time. Troops were raised by private people, and Oliver Cromwell found himself in command of a troop of horses. Together with his parliamentary friends he was present at the first battle against the king. The king, helped by his fiery nephew, Prince Rupert, fresh over from the Thirty Years' War, was victorious. Cromwell knew why.

"Your troops," he said to one of his friends, "are old decayed serving-men, and the king's troops are gentlemen's sons. Do you think that the spirits of such base and mean fellows will ever be able to encounter gentlemen, that have honour and courage and resolution in them?"

The final result of the whole war lay in these words. Cromwell now chose men for the army who were sternly Puritan, who had their hearts in the cause, who had some conscience in what they did. Every soldier henceforth had to undergo a severe training. Cromwell himself, having learned from a Dutchman the art of war, drilled the men, until he had a cavalry regiment under his orders so fiery with zeal, so well restrained, that no body of horse could compare with it. No longer was there any thought of flight, none of retreat; deeds of eternal fame were done, endless and infinite. 'From that day forward they were never beaten.' So Cromwell and his Ironsides, as the soldiers were called, advanced to victory. Red coats were worn for the first time in this 'New Model Army', as it was called.

The king was finally beaten and brought to trial in London. Then came the signing of the death-warrant by Cromwell and fifty-seven others, and preparations for the execution. The dignity which had failed the poor king in his life, came to him in these last days. He was allowed to say good-bye to his young children, a scene among the most pathetic in history. Having taken them on his knee and kissed them again and yet again, he ordered them to be taken away. When they reached the door they flew back to his arms, sobbing aloud, until the wretched King Charles tore himself away, only to fall on his knees in prayer. 50

Firmly he mounted the scaffold. As his head was lifted up to the sight of his subjects, a groan of pity and horror burst from the crowd. The news was received throughout Europe in silent horror. 55

But the death of the king was a great landmark in history. The old rule was behind, the new rule was before. A new life had arisen for England, which would affect the history of Europe. 60

Oliver Cromwell was now a king in all but name. Of his campaigns in Ireland and Scotland there is no time to tell. At the age of forty-three he had girt on his sword. At the age of fifty-two he laid it down.

"See what a multitude of people come to attend your triumph," they said to him when he returned from the wars. 65

"More would come to see me hanged," he had answered with a careless smile, knowing how unpopular he was.

The country had been torn by war for ten years. Cromwell now turned his attention to a settlement of affairs. And first and foremost came the Act giving to the English increased power at sea, with more far-reaching results than even Oliver Cromwell could foresee. 70

Cromwell had conquered all upon the land. He now turned to the sea, and tried to improve the trade of England by stopping the Dutch ships from bringing so much goods to English shores. No longer now could Dutch ships carry corn from Russia to England; no longer could they fish so freely for herrings off the English coast to take to Germany and other countries. No longer could they be the chief carriers of Europe, 'waggoners of the sea'. The ships of England were to take their own share of the world's sea-traffic. 75

From olden days England had claimed her right over the English Channel.

"It is the custom of the English to command at sea," the king used to say with pride. Indeed up to this time the flags of all other countries had been lowered before the flag of England while sailing through the narrow English Channel. 80

One day – it was in the year 1651 – a Dutch fleet passed through the Channel without lowering the flag in salute to an English ship which it passed. The English admiral asked the reason of this insult, and as the Dutch captain refused to explain, he captured the flagship. 85

Relations now became very strained between the two countries. War was not yet declared, when suddenly one day the Dutch admiral, Tromp, sailed into the English Channel and anchored off the south coast with forty ships.

From *The Awakening of Europe* by M.B. Synge

Answer the following questions.

1 What caused war to break out between the Dutch and the British?

_____

2 Why do you think that a story about the four-year-old Oliver beating the younger Prince Charles at 'fisticuffs' has been included?

_____

_____

_____

3 What prompted Cromwell to take a more active role in government?

_____

_____

4 Explain why Cromwell lost his first battle against the king.

_____

_____

_____

_____

5 Describe the ways in which Cromwell revolutionised his army.

_____

_____

_____

_____

6 How did Cromwell ensure that his army stayed motivated?

_____

_____

7 Explain why the 'New Model Army' was an effective name for Cromwell's men.

_____

_____

_____

8 Find an example of a **metaphor** in the text.

_____

9 Give an alternative for each word as it is used in the text.

   a pathetic (line 51) _____   **b** sorry (line 18) _____

   c steeped (line 7) _____

10 Explain, in your own words, how Cromwell tried to improve trade and how this approach could work. Refer to the text in your answer.

_____

_____

_____

_____

_____

_____

11 Use the information given in the text to write a character description of Cromwell as an adult.

_____

_____

_____

_____

_____

_____

12 Explain each of the following phrases, as used in the text.

   a '…base and mean fellows…' (lines 34–35) _____

   b '…deeds of eternal fame were done…' (line 43) _____

   c '…he had girt on his sword…' (line 62) _____

13 Do you think that the writer admires Cromwell? Support your answer with FIVE pieces of evidence.

_____

_____

_____

_____

_____

_____ 5

Now go to the Progress Chart to record your score!   Total 35

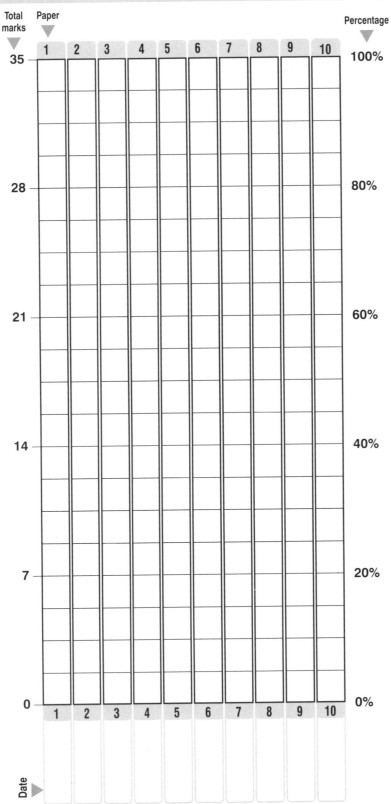